Credit Theory

a complete guide to learning about credit score theory, what it takes to improve it; get your bank loan today.

John Cash - Credit Score Academy

Introduction

The reality is that we live in a society that almost demands that we have some form of credit, not to get ahead, but simply to survive. When we are without it, we suffer in more ways than one.

What better reason is there to start mending our financial health than this? Yes, it can be scary, unpredictable, and stressful but by applying the strategies outlined in this book, you can find your way to a successful credit repair without the additional expense of hiring services to do it for you.

There is an excellent benefit to fixing your credit yourself. Not only do you save yourself from an additional expense when you are already financially strapped, but you become an expert and play a major starring role in your own life.

By applying the information in this book, you will have enough resources at your disposal to get your finances back on track. They say that it takes three weeks for you to get into long-lasting habits. When you are able to budget and watch how you spend, you will quickly find yourself developing new habits.

This guidebook will cover all of the tips and tricks that you need to know in order to get to know about credit scores. You can utilize these administrations if you are worried about wholesale fraud, or when you are building your credit profile and you have to screen your advancement. If your requirement for a credit card score is easygoing, you don't have to leave behind month-to-month expenses to pay for an observing help.

What is the credit score?

Credit score is the number derived after analyzing a person's financial records, particularly his credit history, to determine his creditworthiness level. It is a number that represents how well that person handles all the money that he borrows. It is the main determinant used by many lending companies, next to or together with the five C's of credit (character, capacity, capital, collateral, conditions). While the latter determines the creditworthiness of a person, the former objectively interprets it. Most companies use numerous credit assessment measures to assess their potential borrowers' creditworthiness, but the credit score stands to be the most objective of all. Credit scores help many institutions in making financial and corporate decisions. Lending companies such as credit card companies, banks, and other financial institutions use the credit score to determine the possible risks they will face when lending money to a person.

They also use this score to evaluate the possible losses they might experience due to unpaid loans and bad debts. They also use this score to determine who are qualified to be their borrowers, the amount they will lend to them, the different terms and conditions that they may impose for each of them, and the interest rate they can charge to them.

For instance, obtaining credit is a person's option whenever he runs out of cash. He can still buy using a credit card issued by the lending company. However, issuing a credit card takes many steps, one of which is assessing his financial capability. The credit score will help lending companies in determining if he is a creditworthy person.

Creditworthiness is the measure of the possibility that a person will pay his financial obligations. Other countries, however, consider creditworthiness as the measure of the possibility that a person will fail to comply with his monetary obligations.

Creditworthiness is important in financial matters because lending companies also have to generate revenue from lending money. Suppose they do not check the creditworthiness of each of their borrowers. In that case, they may find themselves in bankruptcy either because their borrowers are cashless or because they already have left the country. Creditworthiness serves as a means to protect the interest not only of the lending company, but also of the public.

What's good credit score?

The main document used by lending companies in computing a person's credit score is the credit report. It contains various personal and financial information of the individual such as the place they live, the specific manner through which they pay their bills, their current financial condition (whether they are currently bankrupt or insolvent), and whether they been sued for collection of money due to unpaid loans. Obtaining a credit report is free, so before a person applies for credit, they must get a copy of it. The Fair Credit Reporting Act (FCRA), the law governing the reporting of a person's credit information, requires every credit reporting company or agency to provide a person a free copy of their credit report once every year at their request.

What's the fico score?

You have heard it again and again, your FICO score must be so high to get this type of credit, this kind of interest rate, and this type of privilege. The FICO score is the single most important factor that stands between you and just about anything you want to get. While many people fully understand the impact of the FICO score on their credit, few people, if asked, could actually tell you what it is or how it is determined. Given the weight that this number holds over so many people, it seems amazing that more people don't ask what it is or what they can do about it. They just simply accept the fact that this number has so much power in their lives.

Most people do not realize that the credit bureau that issues your reports does not determine your score, it is done by another company, a third party called the Fair, Isaac Corporation (FICO). They weigh all the different elements of your credit report to determine what number you get. All the data collected by the credit bureaus are factored in to come up with a three-digit number.

Almost every creditor will want to see your FICO score before he decides to give you credit. But knowing what the numbers really mean can make a huge difference in managing and taking back control of your financial future. As you gain more knowledge about how the system works, it can empower you. While other factors will weigh in the decision, anyone whose goal is to improve their creditworthiness needs to start with the FICO score as nearly all credit decisions will be based on it.

One of the first things you should understand is the scoring range so you can see what your number really means.

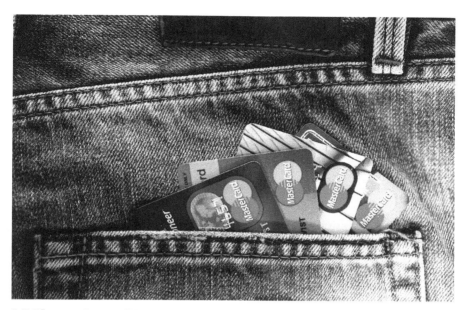

Why Is Fico Score Important?

This is probably the only grade you should seriously worry about after you get out of school. It is the grade you get for your financial stability. That single three-digit number will tell the world what they should think about you. But it is not a number that reflects only the present it is also a pathway to your future as well. If anything is wrong with your reports, it is your responsibility to get it fixed. This is the primary and most effective way to change it.

For this reason, it is important that you know what's in your report so that you can correct any information that is incorrect or incomplete. This will help to bring your score up higher. Very few people have a perfect score of 950, but you can improve that number if you know what to do.

The Difference Between FICO and Other Credit Scores

The reason for this is that FICO scores will be seen as the standard when it comes to making fair and accurate decisions about an individual's creditworthiness.

Now there are other credit scores out there, and they can be used in some situations. These other scores will calculate the number they give you differently than the FICO score can. So, while it may seem like some of those other scores are similar to what we see with the FICO score, they aren't. Only FICO scores will be used by most of the top lenders you want to borrow from, and while the others can be good for some monitoring of your score, if you would like, the best way to go is with the FICO score.

There are different scores that lenders can get from the different bureaus and the score for one may not mean the same thing as the other. This is important because when you get your credit score, it is imperative that you know exactly what your number means and if you're in hot water or not. There are different credit scoring ranges for different lenders. Here are the most popular ones:

FICO Credit Scoring Range

Extension of Range: 350-850 is the credit score range. The Fair Isaac Corporation's credit score is what many lenders see when they look at your credit report.

This score is one of the most used out there. The FICO score shows how creditworthy you are in the eyes of lenders.

There's not just one type of FICO score as new next generation/NextGen scores have been introduced that go up to 950.

Vantage Score Credit Scoring Range

Extension of Range: 501-990. The Vantage Score credit scoring model is formed by the 3 major credit bureaus, namely TransUnion, Equifax and Experian.

When you receive your credit score from one of these bureaus directly, they will most likely give you this Vantage Score. It is also referred to as the Vantage Score 2.0 model.

Vantage Scores 3.0 Credit Scoring Range

Extension of Range: 300-850. This credit scoring model is largely similar to the previous one (Vantage Score 2.0 Model). The only big difference is that the range is slightly larger for the Vantage Score 3.0 Range, i.e. 300-850.

Trans Risk Credit Scoring Range

Extension of Range: 300-850. This range is used by the credit bureau Trans Union when they are trying to pin your creditworthiness down.

Equifax Credit Scoring Range

Extension of Range: 280-850. This is the scoring range used by the credit bureau Equifax, to show how risky it is to lend to you.

Experian Plus Credit Scoring Range

Extension of Range: 330-830. This one is used by the credit bureau Experian and is how that credit bureau shows how creditworthy you are.

How Is Fico Score Calculated?

When your FICO score is determined, several factors must be taken into consideration. The actual score is calculated based on their order of importance.

35% is based on your payment history. As long as you pay your bills on time, this part of your score will be high.

30% is based on how much money you owe. It is called your credit utilization ratio. While you want to be using your credit, you don't want to be using 100% of it. When you are maxed out credit wise, it can have an impact on how high your score will be. Try to aim to spend no more than 30% of your total credit limit to get an optimal balance.

15% is based on your credit

history. The longer you have had credit, the better.

10% is based on the different types of credit you have. A nice combination is always good to see. If you have credit card debt, a mortgage, and installment loans, it shows that you are versatile when it comes to credit and you can handle all sorts of things responsibility.

10% is based on new credit. You don't want to go out and apply for a bunch of loans to get new credit, but if you have some new credit, it looks very positive and could have a positive effect on your score.

Having information like this can go a long way in helping you to see what kind of things actually are involved in determining your credit score. As you can see, all of it is important but being able to see exactly where your weak points are can give you a specific target area you can focus on improving.

No one knows the exact formula for calculating a credit score. The Fair Isaacs Corporation is pretty tight-lipped when asked about the specific algorithms they use. However, as you can see from the above, much of the weight is based on your payment history. That's why it is so important that you find a way to pay your bills as soon as they come due. By doing this, you can be sure that you'll have a leg up when it comes to repairing your credit.

Why should i care about having good credit?

When you apply for credit, insurance, telephone service and even a place to live, providers want to know if you have a good risk level. And to make that decision, they use credit scores.

A credit score is a number. A high score means you have good credit. A low score means you have bad credit.

A higher score means that you represent a lower risk and are more likely to get the product or service - or pay less.

It works as follows: Credit managers extract information from your credit reports, such as your bill payment history, your accounts' age, your unpaid debts and the collection actions initiated against you.

Credit scores can be used in various ways. These are some examples.

- **Insurance companies** use the information in your credit report and combine it with other factors to predict the probability that you present an insurance claim and predict the amount you could claim. They consider this information to decide if they will grant you insurance and how much they will charge you.

- .**Public service companies** use credit scores to decide if they will require a new customer deposit to provide the service. Cell phone providers and homeowners who rent homes also use scores when considering a new client or tenant.

Each type of company has different scoring systems, and credit scoring models can also be based on other information apart from your credit report's data. For example, when you apply for a mortgage loan, the system can consider the amount of the advance, the total amount of your debts and your income.

Access to best credit cards

Having a good credit score is an essential factor to qualify for an opportunity to get a credit card that provides excellent cash-back reward programs, awesome advantages, low rates and so many others. Besides paying lower interest and fees, having access to the best credit card means you can get a larger credit limit. Therefore, you can have freedom and flexibility to make purchases you want without the financial constraint that arises from a small credit limit.

An increase in your credit limit results into an increase in your creditworthiness overtime. This shows banks and other lending institutions that you are mature enough and can handle the responsibility of having access to a large amount of credit.

Having a good credit score can help you discover cards with cash-back rates as high as 5% at different places like restaurants, grocery stores, E-commerce platforms, gas stations and any other time your card is used.

Easy access to loan

Having a bad credit history will make you scared of applying for a new credit card or loan due to the fear of being turned down. Maintaining a good credit score tells a lot about your credit responsibility. When banks and lending institution see your credit score, they can be rest assured that they are not at risk and you are likely to pay back the money you are asking them to loan to you. Though this does not guarantee an outright approval because other factors such as your income, debts, etc. are also considered, it just provides you with a very good chance of getting approval.

Lower interest rates on loans

The interest rate that you get to pay is directly dependent on your credit score. Suppose you have a very good credit score. In that case, you might not need to consider the interest rate when applying for a credit card because you will always qualify for the best interest rates thereby paying very minimal charges on credit card loans. If you always want your interest rate to be low, you need to have a good credit score.

Easy approval for rental of houses and apartment

So many landlords and apartment owners tend to check credit scores for the same reason lenders do routinely. They fear that tenants with bad credit score might be unable to keep up with rent payment and avoid the hassle – they avoid tenants with a high risk. Having previous bad credit scores gives the property owner an unsettled mind that you might not be able to pay back at the stipulated time, a good credit score says otherwise.

Better job applications

This is not the only criteria considered by employers, however, so many employers access the credit history of various job seekers during their application processes especially when the job you're applying for requires handling money or accessing clients' sensitive financial information. Majority of employers believe that your ability to use credit responsibly makes you more likely to be a responsible employee.

Negotiating Power

You can get leverage to negotiate a lower interest rate on your student loan, new credit card, mortgage and others if you have a good credit score. Having a credit card with a history that doesn't have an iota of problems provides you with more bargaining power, that is needed to secure the favorable terms that you need. You therefore can carefully pick the terms that will be of great advantage to your present financial circumstance.

What is in a credit report?

There are a lot of different categories in the report and that means you need to weigh out different things to make sure that your credit score is high enough for you to get the things you want.

The best scores are those that are over 900 but not many people are able to achieve that. If your score is over a 700 you have good credit and you're pretty much guaranteed any type of credit that you might apply for. But you want to keep in mind that different types of credit card companies or credit

agencies will want a different score.

If your score is in the 600's you have a decent chance of getting credit in most places but not all. This isn't guaranteed, however. There are plenty of agencies that will consider you a little bit of a risk.

Your credit score is an indication of how much of a risk it is to give you credit. When you first start out getting credit you have a low credit score. This tells the person checking your score that there is a high level of risk involved. That's why your score is low. As you get more recorded payments your score will go up because the risk of you not paying for things is getting lower.

Now it's not just late payments or missed payments that will count against you in regard to your credit score.

So, let's break them down a little and look at what's on your credit report.

These are the worst things you can have, judgments and tax liens against you. Any of these will make a big dent in your credit score and they will continue to work against you for a very long time (up to 7 years). You don't want these if you can help it.

The next thing is your credit items. These are credit cards, loans, mortgages and any other credit account that you've had in the past. Most accounts that are considered old (closed more than 10 years ago) will not report unless you've had a collection filed for that account.

Every on-time payment will count in your

favor and every late payment, missed payment or collection will count against you. Each balance is reported as well and high balances will also count against you.

Remember we said before that you want to have a high available credit balance, but you also want to have a low balance on the credit you're using. What the credit reporting agency does is look at how much you're able to spend on all of your credit cards and add that together. That's your available credit balance. They then look at how much money you owe on each of those cards and add that all together.

The amount owed is divided by the amount available and that's your total balance percentage. You want to keep this percentage low because that reflects well on your credit card. A high percentage will look bad and lower your credit score.

The total amount of accounts that you have as well as the types of accounts will count towards your score as well. You want to have a moderate number of accounts (more than 10) as long as you can keep them all current.

Finally, the number of inquiries that you have will affect your score. You want to cut down on the amount of inquiries that you have because everyone is a slight ding to your account. What these are is every time that you apply for credit. That's why you want to apply for credit infrequently and only if you're sure you will get it. Getting the credit will help improve your score more than it will hurt for the inquiry.

- You want to make sure of a few important things in regard to your credit report:
- Have several different accounts (10 or more)?
- Keep all accounts current
- Avoid public records
- Keep your available balance high
- Keep the balance in use low
- Don't apply for credit unless necessary
- Never apply for credit unless you're sure you'll be approved
- Dispute accounts that aren't correct
- Make payments on any past due accounts and pay off collections

By doing all of these things your credit score will increase over time. It will take some time and you will need to work at it, but you'll be able to bring your credit score back up. Once you're able to bring your score back up, you'll find it even easier to get out of debt and you'll start saving better as well. The reason your credit score will affect this is because your credit score has a lot to do with you getting approved for everything from credit cards to car loans to housing. It also has to do with the interest rates that you're given. Staying out of debt means you have more money to put away towards your savings. it's a win all the way around.

Credit Reporting Agencies

There are three fundamental consumer announcing agencies: Trans-Union, Equifax, and Experian (in the past known as T.R.W.). These three significant information agencies have a lock on the revealing credit industry and summarize more than 90 percent of the credit report information in the United States. Because every one of the three agencies is rivaling one another for a similar customer base, they are incredibly serious with each other and don't share information. The rivalry has driven these agencies to extend their districts. The agencies currently give Information to supporters all through the world. The agencies are benefit situated, with profits originating from the people and businesses who buy into them as their hotspot for consumer information. Remember that a consumer detailing organization is decided on the painstaking quality, practicality, and precision of the consumer information it assembles. The way that the agencies don't impart Information to each other is both a gift and a revile. For instance, one report shows every single great record; you are fit as a fiddle. However, if another report shows an awful record, you are in a difficult situation. Many businesses and organizations buy into more than one credit detailing office to abstain from making expensive mistakes in deciding an individual's credit value. As clarified, the agencies get businesses and organizations to buy into them by demonstrating that their credit reports and credit files are the most accurate and complete Information accessible on the consumer (you and me).

The best credit organization is the one that re-ports both negative and positive Information with practicality and precision. Businesses and organizations depend intensely upon the practicality and exactness of the Information when endeavoring to settle on a qualified choice concerning credit value. Credit agencies should report truthful Information concerning foundation information and consumer credit propensities. Since credit agencies start announcing your experience information and consumer credit propensities from your first credit understanding, it is essential to build up or restore a strong consumer establishment at a convenient time. However, setting up and restoring isn't constantly a simple task to embrace. Realizing where to turn and what to search for is critical to beginning on the correct foot. So you ask how would I build up or restore my's-self as a capable credit-utilizing consumer? How about we investigate only a couple of thoughts that can be useful to you as a dependable credit consumer.

Where Do Agencies Get Information?

There are a large number of credit agencies situated all through the United States. A credit organization's fundamental capacity is to accumulate Information on you and put that information into a report called a credit report or a consumer report. A credit report is an archive that contains an accurate record of a person's consumer credit payment history. The report is generated by the credit organization and is only one of the snippets of Information used by an outsider to decide a person's credit value. We should note here for the future that a credit report is different from a consumer file. A consumer file is an assortment of the entirety of the Information assembled on a person by a credit organization. Your credit report is a changeless piece of your consumer file. The Fair Credit Reporting Act is a bit of enactment that administers what credit agencies can and can't get to.

A credit report must bear on a consumer's credit value, credit standing, credit limit, character, general reputation, personal qualities, or method of living." So, by definition, credit agencies have a wide range from which they can accumulate Information on you. Remember that each

part of your consumer life and certain regions of your private life are available to the credit agencies. A case of the sort of Information a credit organization can put in your credit file and on your credit report is the act of composing terrible checks. The composition of an awful check thinks about your general reputation. If a business reports the composition of a terrible check to a credit office, the credit organization has the option to put that information in your consumer file and on your credit report. Since you recognize what kinds of Information the credit agencies can accumulate, you presently need to know from whom they can get the Information. Credit agencies accumulate the Information they need from businesses, organizations, open and private sources, and legislative workplaces. These are similar businesses, organizations, open and private sources, and legislative workplaces that you use consistently. The credit agencies request spots of business, promising complete and accurate credit information—this is how a credit office is judged. When the position of the business is joined with a credit organization, the two offer information about you that is crucial to the two. The entirety of the groups requested by the credit agencies depends upon the fulfillment and precision of the Information accumulated to help them in choices, including a person's credit value.

What's a Good Credit Score?

In the current economy, it's a lot harder to qualify for a loan. Presently you need an excellent credit score to qualify for most types of credit. So what's a good credit score rating?

850 is immaculate credit and the most elevated credit score rating conceivable; however, I've never personally observed anybody with an 850. A good credit score begins in the 670 territory. Scores lower than 670 are not viewed as good credit.

In general, credit score values range from 300 to 850. A lower value means that a person is less creditworthy, while a higher value means that he is more creditworthy. However, this interpretation is broadened by the lending companies using their respective financial data on their clients. Instead of referring to a high or a low credit score, they have developed certain brackets that explain how creditworthy a person is. The following explains what each range of credit scores mean:

- A credit score of 751 to 800 allows a borrower to apply for credit with the lowest interest rate and the most competitive amount because the lending companies have an assurance that he will not default in his monetary obligations. Many consider this score as the best. Someone who gets a score within this range can be almost certain their application will be granted.

- A credit score of 711 to 750 allows a borrower to apply for credit at competitive interest rates. While the person's credit standing is relatively good, a slightly higher interest rate would be charged to them compared to someone who scores 751 and up. Someone who scores at this range gets a relatively good credit standing.

- A credit score of 651 to 710 allows a borrower to apply for credit at moderate interest rates. This is the normal score that applicants must get to ensure that their application will be granted.

- A credit score of 581-650 may be allowed to apply for credit, but he must obtain it at high interest rates. This is because at this range, the possibility of risks and loses is getting high.
- A credit score of 300-580 does not allow a person to apply for credit. Their application may be granted, but they can only avail it if they are willing to pay the highest interest rate. This is because at this range, possibility of losses is very high.

However, one must take note that there is no general method in determining the credit score of a person. Its computation depends on the company assessing him. His credit score may be different when assessed by different companies, but also the range of scores may be interpreted to mean the same thing because of the elements considered in assessing him.

For instance, his score may be 375 in one company and 340 in another, but both scores mean that he is less creditworthy and has to repair his credit score fast.

Conclusion

After reading this plan you have to come up with a financial plan which will help you start to pay off your credit cards strategically. You then have to make sure that, no matter what, you follow this plan. Even if you find yourself in an emergency after a few months when your car breaks down, you should find another way to come up with your emergency funding. It is important that you continue to make more than the minimum payment on time with all your credit cards. The fewer fees you need to add into your balance, the quicker you will be able to pay off your credit card debt.

Another way to bring down credit card debt quickly, especially if you are overdrawn and missed a few payments, is to contact the credit card company. While many people don't realize this, most credit card companies want to work with you. The number one reason for this is they want to keep you as a customer, basically, so they can continue receiving your money. One strategy to use is to call and say that you would like to close your account. They will then try to focus on keeping your account open, which usually results in them dropping a few missed payment or over the limit fees. Another strategy to use is simply to explain to them what happened, why you were late, and tell them that you want to put your account in good standing. They are usually willing to drop some fees or so much money if you are willing to pay a certain amount off that day.

Don't hesitate, put all the notions of the book into practice immediately and improve your credit score!

CPSIA information can be obtained
at www.ICGtesting.com
Printed in the USA
BVHW080128280421
605943BV00008B/949